Copyright © 2024 Chimezie Igwe

All rights reserved

The characters and events portrayed in this book are fictitious. Any similarity to real persons, living or dead, is coincidental and not intended by the author.

No part of this book may be reproduced, or stored in a retrieval system, or transmitted in any form or by any means, electronic, mechanical, photocopying, recording, or otherwise, without express written permission of the publisher.

ISBN: 9798321736234
Imprint: Independently published

Cover design by: Art Painter
Library of Congress Control Number: 2018675309
Printed in the United States of America

"Love knows no bounds in the digital age, where screens become windows to the heart, and connections transcend the limitations of distance."

CHIMEZIE IGWE

CONTENTS

Copyright
Epigraph
Preface
Chapter 1   1
Unveiling the Digital Romance Renaissance   2
Navigating the Technicolor Tapestry of Love   3
Crafting Your Digital Love Story   4
Navigating the Digital Dating Landscape   5
Love in the Time of Screens: A Digital Romance Manifesto   6
Chapter 2   7
Unlocking the Gates of Digital Romance   8
Decoding the Digital Language of Love   9
Navigating the Digital Dating Minefield   10
The Art of Virtual Courtship   11
Embracing the Adventure of Online Dating   12
Chapter 2   13
Unlocking the Gates of Digital Romance   14
Decoding the Digital Language of Love   15
Navigating the Digital Dating Minefield   16
The Art of Virtual Courtship   17
Embracing the Adventure of Online Dating   18

Chapter 4	19
The Evolution of Digital Discourse	20
The Art of Engaging Dialogue	21
Navigating the Nuances of Virtual Communication	22
Building Bridges, Not Walls	23
Embracing Authenticity and Vulnerability	24
The Power of Presence and Patience	25
Chapter 5	26
The Rise of Virtual Intimacy	27
Creating a Virtual Sanctuary	28
The Art of Engaging Conversation	29
Nurturing Emotional Connection	30
Exploring Shared Activities	31
The Power of Presence and Patience	32
Embracing the Journey	33
Chapter 6	34
Navigating the Transition	35
Setting the Stage for Success	36
Managing Expectations	37
The First Meeting: Making a Memorable Impression	38
Navigating the Dynamics of In-Person Interaction	39
Embracing the Journey	40
Chapter 7	41
Navigating the Transition	42
Cultivating Connection	43
Communication is Key	44
Embracing Vulnerability	45
Navigating Digital Distractions	46

Cultivating Gratitude	47
Embracing Growth and Change	48
The Power of Rituals	49
Embracing the Journey	50
Chapter 8	51
The Digital Love Story	52
Navigating the Digital Playground	53
The Power of Connection	54
Embracing Authenticity	55
The Pitfalls of Perfection	56
Navigating Digital Boundaries	57
The Future of Digital Romance	58
Embracing the Journey	59
Chapter 9	60
Embracing the Digital Romance	61
The Importance of Connection	62
Navigating the Challenges	63
The Power of Love	64
Embracing the Journey	65

PREFACE

Welcome to the world of digital romance, where love transcends geographical boundaries and flourishes amidst the pixels of screens. In an era defined by technology and connectivity, the landscape of relationships has undergone a profound transformation, offering new opportunities and challenges for seekers of love and connection. This book is a comprehensive guide designed to navigate the complexities of modern romance in the digital age, offering insights, strategies, and practical advice for fostering authentic connections and meaningful relationships in the digital realm. Whether you're swiping right on dating apps, navigating the nuances of online communication, or nurturing a long-distance love affair through video calls, this book will equip you with the tools and knowledge you need to thrive in the ever-evolving world of digital romance. So, dear reader, join us on this journey as we explore the intricacies of love, connection, and intimacy in the digital era, and discover the magic that lies within the pixels of screens.

CHAPTER 1
The Digital Age of Love: Where Pixels Pulse with Passion

Welcome to the digital age, where love takes on new dimensions, and connections transcend the physical realm. In this chapter, we'll embark on a journey through the landscape of modern romance, exploring how technology has reshaped the way we love, flirt, and form meaningful connections. So, buckle up and get ready to dive deep into the digital sea of love!

UNVEILING THE DIGITAL ROMANCE RENAISSANCE

Imagine yourself in a bustling coffee shop, surrounded by the chatter of patrons and the aroma of freshly brewed coffee. Amid this scene, you're not alone; your smartphone is nestled in your palm, a gateway to a world of romantic possibilities. This is the digital age of love—a time where swiping right or sending a heart emoji can spark a connection that transcends boundaries.

Gone are the days of waiting by the phone for a potential suitor to call; in today's world, love is just a click away. With dating apps and social media platforms at our fingertips, we have the power to connect with people from all walks of life, forging bonds that would have been impossible in the pre-digital era.

But what lies beyond the glossy veneer of digital romance? Is it possible to find true love amidst the sea of profiles and pixels? The answer, dear reader, is a resounding yes. In the digital age, love knows no bounds, and the possibilities for connection are endless.

NAVIGATING THE TECHNICOLOR TAPESTRY OF LOVE

In the digital age, love is no longer confined to the boundaries of geography or social circles. With the rise of online dating platforms and social media networks, we have the opportunity to connect with potential partners from around the globe, each profile a window into a world of romance and adventure.

But with this newfound freedom comes a dizzying array of choices, each one more tantalizing than the last. From niche dating apps catering to specific interests to mainstream platforms boasting millions of users, the digital landscape of love is as diverse as it is vast.

So, how do we navigate this technicolor tapestry of love? How do we find our way amidst the sea of profiles and possibilities? The key, dear reader, is to approach digital romance with an open heart and a discerning eye. While the allure of endless options may be tempting, it's important to stay true to ourselves and our values, seeking connections that resonate with our deepest desires and aspirations.

CRAFTING YOUR DIGITAL LOVE STORY

At the heart of every successful digital romance lies authenticity—the courage to be vulnerable, to be true to ourselves, and to let our true selves shine through. In a world where filters and facades often reign supreme, authenticity is the secret ingredient that sets our profiles apart from the crowd, attracting genuine connections that stand the test of time.

Consider the story of Alex and Emma, two twenty-somethings who met through a popular dating app. Instead of crafting a profile filled with clichés and platitudes, Alex took the time to showcase his true personality, sharing his love for hiking, photography, and 90s sitcoms with potential matches. Emma, impressed by Alex's authenticity and humor, reached out with a witty message that sparked a conversation that would ultimately lead to their first date—and the beginning of a beautiful romance.

NAVIGATING THE DIGITAL DATING LANDSCAPE

In the digital age, the rules of romance are constantly evolving, and it's easy to feel overwhelmed by the endless stream of profiles and possibilities. But fear not, dear reader, for I'm here to be your digital love guru, offering sage advice and thoughtful guidance as you navigate the choppy waters of modern romance.

Let's start by discussing the dos and don'ts of online dating etiquette. From crafting the perfect opening message to navigating the murky waters of ghosting and rejection, there's a lot to consider when it comes to digital courtship. But with a little patience, persistence, and a healthy dose of optimism, you can find the love of your life in the digital sea of possibilities.

LOVE IN THE TIME OF SCREENS: A DIGITAL ROMANCE MANIFESTO

As we navigate the digital age of love, let's remember that behind every profile and pixel lies a beating heart—a soul searching for connection, companionship, and love. Whether you're swiping through profiles on a dating app or chatting with a potential match in a virtual chatroom, let's approach each interaction with kindness, compassion, and an open heart.

And remember, dear reader, that love knows no bounds in the digital age. So, embrace the adventure, seize the moment, and let your heart lead the way as you embark on your own digital love story. The journey may be unpredictable, and the path may be winding, but in the end, love always finds a way, even in the time of screens.

CHAPTER 2
The Digital Matchmaker: Online Dating

In the vast and ever-evolving landscape of the digital age, one phenomenon stands out as a beacon of hope and opportunity for singles worldwide: online dating. In this chapter, we will delve into the intricate world of digital matchmaking, exploring the nuances of online dating platforms, decoding the dos and don'ts of creating an engaging profile, and unraveling the mysteries of virtual courtship. So, fasten your seatbelts as we embark on a journey through the virtual realm of love and romance!

UNLOCKING THE GATES OF DIGITAL ROMANCE

Picture this: you're lounging on your couch, sipping a cup of tea, and contemplating your love life. In the past, meeting potential partners was limited to chance encounters at social events or introductions by mutual friends. But in today's digital age, the game has changed. With the click of a button, you can access a vast array of online dating platforms, each promising to connect you with your perfect match.

From traditional websites like Match.com to trendy apps like Tinder and Bumble, the options are endless. Whether you're seeking a serious relationship or a casual fling, there's a platform out there to suit your needs. But with great power comes great responsibility, and navigating the world of online dating requires a keen understanding of its intricacies.

Online dating has become a global phenomenon, transcending geographical boundaries and cultural barriers. It has democratized the dating scene, offering opportunities for connection to individuals who may not have crossed paths otherwise. This democratization has led to a diverse pool of potential partners, allowing individuals to explore their options and find someone who truly resonates with them.

DECODING THE DIGITAL LANGUAGE OF LOVE

Creating an online dating profile is akin to crafting a personal brand—it's your opportunity to showcase your best self to potential matches. But in a sea of profiles vying for attention, how do you stand out from the crowd? The key lies in authenticity, dear reader. Be genuine, be yourself, and let your unique personality shine through in every word and photo.

Think of your profile as a window into your soul—a glimpse into your interests, passions, and aspirations. Instead of resorting to clichés and generic phrases, take the time to craft a profile that reflects who you truly are. Share anecdotes from your life, highlight your hobbies and interests, and don't be afraid to inject a bit of humor and wit into your bio. After all, laughter is often the best icebreaker!

Your profile picture plays a crucial role in attracting potential matches. Choose a photo that accurately represents you and showcases your personality. Whether you're posing with your beloved pet, participating in your favorite hobby, or simply smiling at the camera, make sure your picture is clear, flattering, and inviting. Remember, first impressions are key in the world of online dating!

NAVIGATING THE DIGITAL DATING MINEFIELD

Once your profile is live, brace yourself for an influx of messages, likes, and matches. But don't let the attention overwhelm you—navigating the digital dating minefield requires a steady hand and a discerning eye. As you sift through potential matches, keep an open mind and be willing to step outside your comfort zone.

When it comes to initiating conversations, a little creativity can go a long way. Instead of resorting to tired pickup lines or generic greetings, take the time to craft a personalized message that shows genuine interest in your match's profile. Ask about their hobbies, compliment their photos, or share a funny anecdote from your own life. Remember, the goal is to spark a meaningful conversation that lays the foundation for a deeper connection.

Engaging in meaningful conversations is key to building rapport and establishing a connection with your potential matches. Ask open-ended questions that invite thoughtful responses, share personal anecdotes, and be genuinely curious about your match's interests and experiences. Remember, communication is the cornerstone of any successful relationship, and investing time and effort into getting to know your match can set the stage for a meaningful connection.

THE ART OF VIRTUAL COURTSHIP

As your conversations progress, you may find yourself drawn to certain individuals who resonate with your values and interests. Congratulations—you've entered the realm of virtual courtship! In this digital dance of attraction, communication is key. Take the time to get to know your match on a deeper level, asking thoughtful questions and sharing personal anecdotes from your own life.

But beware of the pitfalls that lurk in the digital dating landscape. From catfishing to ghosting, online dating can be fraught with challenges. Stay vigilant, trust your instincts, and never hesitate to block or report anyone who makes you feel uncomfortable or unsafe.

As you navigate the world of online dating, remember to prioritize your safety and well-being above all else. Take precautions when meeting someone for the first time, such as choosing a public location and informing a friend or family member of your plans. Trust your instincts and listen to your gut —if something feels off, don't hesitate to remove yourself from the situation.

EMBRACING THE ADVENTURE OF ONLINE DATING

In the digital age, love knows no bounds, and online dating offers a tantalizing glimpse into the infinite possibilities of romance. So, embrace the adventure, dear reader. Swipe right, send that first message, and open yourself up to the countless opportunities that await you in the virtual realm of love and romance.

But remember, online dating is just one piece of the puzzle. True love transcends the digital realm, blossoming in the real world through shared experiences, laughter, and genuine connection. So, as you navigate the world of online dating, keep your heart open to the possibility of finding love in unexpected places. After all, you never know where the digital matchmaker may lead you next.

CHAPTER 2
The Digital Matchmaker: Online Dating

In the vast and ever-evolving landscape of the digital age, one phenomenon stands out as a beacon of hope and opportunity for singles worldwide: online dating. In this chapter, we will delve into the intricate world of digital matchmaking, exploring the nuances of online dating platforms, decoding the dos and don'ts of creating an engaging profile, and unraveling the mysteries of virtual courtship. So, fasten your seatbelts as we embark on a journey through the virtual realm of love and romance!

UNLOCKING THE GATES OF DIGITAL ROMANCE

Picture this: you're lounging on your couch, sipping a cup of tea, and contemplating your love life. In the past, meeting potential partners was limited to chance encounters at social events or introductions by mutual friends. But in today's digital age, the game has changed. With the click of a button, you can access a vast array of online dating platforms, each promising to connect you with your perfect match.

From traditional websites like Match.com to trendy apps like Tinder and Bumble, the options are endless. Whether you're seeking a serious relationship or a casual fling, there's a platform out there to suit your needs. But with great power comes great responsibility, and navigating the world of online dating requires a keen understanding of its intricacies.

Online dating has become a global phenomenon, transcending geographical boundaries and cultural barriers. It has democratized the dating scene, offering opportunities for connection to individuals who may not have crossed paths otherwise. This democratization has led to a diverse pool of potential partners, allowing individuals to explore their options and find someone who truly resonates with them.

DECODING THE DIGITAL LANGUAGE OF LOVE

Creating an online dating profile is akin to crafting a personal brand—it's your opportunity to showcase your best self to potential matches. But in a sea of profiles vying for attention, how do you stand out from the crowd? The key lies in authenticity, dear reader. Be genuine, be yourself, and let your unique personality shine through in every word and photo.

Think of your profile as a window into your soul—a glimpse into your interests, passions, and aspirations. Instead of resorting to clichés and generic phrases, take the time to craft a profile that reflects who you truly are. Share anecdotes from your life, highlight your hobbies and interests, and don't be afraid to inject a bit of humor and wit into your bio. After all, laughter is often the best icebreaker!

Your profile picture plays a crucial role in attracting potential matches. Choose a photo that accurately represents you and showcases your personality. Whether you're posing with your beloved pet, participating in your favorite hobby, or simply smiling at the camera, make sure your picture is clear, flattering, and inviting. Remember, first impressions are key in the world of online dating!

NAVIGATING THE DIGITAL DATING MINEFIELD

Once your profile is live, brace yourself for an influx of messages, likes, and matches. But don't let the attention overwhelm you—navigating the digital dating minefield requires a steady hand and a discerning eye. As you sift through potential matches, keep an open mind and be willing to step outside your comfort zone.

When it comes to initiating conversations, a little creativity can go a long way. Instead of resorting to tired pickup lines or generic greetings, take the time to craft a personalized message that shows genuine interest in your match's profile. Ask about their hobbies, compliment their photos, or share a funny anecdote from your own life. Remember, the goal is to spark a meaningful conversation that lays the foundation for a deeper connection.

Engaging in meaningful conversations is key to building rapport and establishing a connection with your potential matches. Ask open-ended questions that invite thoughtful responses, share personal anecdotes, and be genuinely curious about your match's interests and experiences. Remember, communication is the cornerstone of any successful relationship, and investing time and effort into getting to know your match can set the stage for a meaningful connection.

THE ART OF VIRTUAL COURTSHIP

As your conversations progress, you may find yourself drawn to certain individuals who resonate with your values and interests. Congratulations—you've entered the realm of virtual courtship! In this digital dance of attraction, communication is key. Take the time to get to know your match on a deeper level, asking thoughtful questions and sharing personal anecdotes from your own life.

But beware of the pitfalls that lurk in the digital dating landscape. From catfishing to ghosting, online dating can be fraught with challenges. Stay vigilant, trust your instincts, and never hesitate to block or report anyone who makes you feel uncomfortable or unsafe.

As you navigate the world of online dating, remember to prioritize your safety and well-being above all else. Take precautions when meeting someone for the first time, such as choosing a public location and informing a friend or family member of your plans. Trust your instincts and listen to your gut—if something feels off, don't hesitate to remove yourself from the situation.

EMBRACING THE ADVENTURE OF ONLINE DATING

In the digital age, love knows no bounds, and online dating offers a tantalizing glimpse into the infinite possibilities of romance. So, embrace the adventure, dear reader. Swipe right, send that first message, and open yourself up to the countless opportunities that await you in the virtual realm of love and romance.

But remember, online dating is just one piece of the puzzle. True love transcends the digital realm, blossoming in the real world through shared experiences, laughter, and genuine connection. So, as you navigate the world of online dating, keep your heart open to the possibility of finding love in unexpected places. After all, you never know where the digital matchmaker may lead you next.

CHAPTER 4
From Chatrooms to DMs: Cultivating Meaningful Conversations Online

Welcome to the digital realm of conversation, where words flow freely and connections are forged through the power of dialogue. In this chapter, we'll explore the art of cultivating meaningful conversations online, from the early days of chatrooms to the modern world of direct messages and virtual communication platforms. So, join me as we embark on a journey through the digital landscape of conversation, where every message holds the potential to deepen connections and foster meaningful relationships.

THE EVOLUTION OF DIGITAL DISCOURSE

Before the era of social media and dating apps, there were chatrooms—virtual gathering places where individuals from all walks of life came together to chat, connect, and share their thoughts and experiences. From the humble beginnings of AOL Instant Messenger to the rise of IRC and MSN Messenger, chatrooms were the original digital watering holes where friendships were formed, romances blossomed, and communities thrived.

Fast forward to the present day, and the landscape of digital conversation has undergone a radical transformation. With the advent of social media platforms like Facebook, Instagram, and Twitter, as well as messaging apps like WhatsApp, Telegram, and Discord, how we communicate online has become more diverse, dynamic, and interconnected than ever before.

THE ART OF ENGAGING DIALOGUE

In the digital age, meaningful conversations are the cornerstone of building connections and fostering relationships. Whether you're chatting with a potential romantic interest, catching up with an old friend, or engaging in a lively debate with a stranger on the internet, the art of engaging dialogue lies in listening, empathy, and genuine curiosity.

When engaging in conversations online, it's important to be present, attentive, and responsive to the needs and interests of your conversation partner. Ask open-ended questions that invite thoughtful responses, share personal anecdotes and experiences, and be willing to explore topics that spark your curiosity and ignite your passion.

NAVIGATING THE NUANCES OF VIRTUAL COMMUNICATION

In the fast-paced world of digital communication, it's easy to get swept up in the whirlwind of notifications, messages, and alerts. But amidst the chaos of constant connectivity, it's important to remember the value of meaningful communication and the impact that our words can have on others.

When engaging in conversations online, be mindful of your tone, language, and communication style. Avoid sarcasm, negativity, and confrontational language that can lead to misunderstandings and conflicts. Instead, strive to maintain a positive and respectful demeanor, even in the face of disagreement or differing opinions.

BUILDING BRIDGES, NOT WALLS

In the digital age, conversations have the power to transcend boundaries and bridge divides, connecting individuals from diverse backgrounds and cultures in ways that were once unimaginable. Whether you're forging new friendships, nurturing existing relationships, or seeking out like-minded communities, the key to meaningful communication lies in building bridges, not walls.

Be open-minded, empathetic, and willing to learn from others' perspectives. Celebrate diversity, embrace difference, and seek out opportunities to engage with individuals who challenge and inspire you. Remember, the beauty of conversation lies in its ability to foster understanding, empathy, and connection, even in the vast and often chaotic world of the internet.

EMBRACING AUTHENTICITY AND VULNERABILITY

At the heart of every meaningful conversation lies authenticity—the courage to be vulnerable, to share our thoughts and feelings openly and honestly, and to connect with others on a deeper level. In the digital age, where filters and facades often reign supreme, authenticity is a rare and precious commodity, capable of transforming ordinary conversations into extraordinary moments of connection and intimacy.

So, don't be afraid to let your guard down, dear reader. Share your passions, fears, and dreams with others, and be willing to listen and learn from their experiences in return. In the end, it's our willingness to be authentic and vulnerable with one another that truly sets the stage for meaningful conversations and meaningful relationships to flourish.

THE POWER OF PRESENCE AND PATIENCE

In the digital age, where attention spans are short and distractions are plentiful, the art of meaningful conversation requires patience, presence, and intentionality. So, slow down, dear reader. Take the time to truly listen to others, engage with them in meaningful dialogue, and savor the connections that you forge along the way.

Remember, meaningful conversations are not just about exchanging words; they're about sharing experiences, building relationships, and creating moments of connection that have the power to transform lives. So, embrace the opportunity to engage with others in meaningful dialogue, and let your words be a beacon of light in the vast and often turbulent sea of digital communication.

CHAPTER 5
Virtual Sparks: Nurturing Chemistry Through Video Calls

Welcome to the era of virtual connections, where sparks fly and chemistry ignites through the magic of video calls. In this chapter, we'll delve into the art of nurturing chemistry through virtual interactions, exploring the nuances of video calls as a medium for building meaningful relationships. So, grab your webcam and get ready to embark on a journey through the digital landscape of love and connection.

THE RISE OF VIRTUAL INTIMACY

In the fast-paced world of modern romance, video calls have emerged as a powerful tool for fostering intimacy and connection, allowing individuals to engage in face-to-face conversations from anywhere in the world. Whether you're miles apart or just a few clicks away, video calls offer a unique opportunity to bridge the gap between physical distance and emotional closeness, bringing you closer to your partner in ways that text messages and phone calls simply can't replicate.

CREATING A VIRTUAL SANCTUARY

Before diving into the world of video calls, it's important to set the stage for success by creating a virtual sanctuary where you and your partner can feel comfortable, relaxed, and fully present. Choose a quiet, well-lit space with minimal distractions, and take the time to set up your camera and microphone for optimal audio and video quality. Consider adding personal touches to your surroundings, such as soft lighting, cozy blankets, or meaningful mementos, to create a warm and inviting atmosphere that encourages open communication and vulnerability.

THE ART OF ENGAGING CONVERSATION

Once you're all set up and ready to go, it's time to dive into the heart of the matter: engaging conversation. The key to a successful video call lies in fostering a meaningful dialogue that flows naturally and effortlessly between you and your partner. Start by asking open-ended questions that invite thoughtful responses and encourage deeper exploration of each other's thoughts, feelings, and experiences.

Listen attentively to your partner's responses, and don't be afraid to share your thoughts, feelings, and stories in return. Remember, the beauty of video calls lies in their ability to capture the nuances of facial expressions, body language, and vocal tone, allowing you to connect with your partner on a deeper level and foster intimacy in ways that transcend the limitations of text-based communication.

NURTURING EMOTIONAL CONNECTION

In addition to fostering engaging conversation, video calls offer a unique opportunity to nurture emotional connection and intimacy with your partner. Take the time to express appreciation, affection, and gratitude for each other, and don't hesitate to share your vulnerabilities, fears, and insecurities in a safe and supportive space.

Use gestures, facial expressions, and vocal inflections to convey warmth, empathy, and understanding, and be attentive to your partner's emotional cues and signals. Remember, emotional connection is the foundation of a healthy and fulfilling relationship, and video calls provide the perfect platform for cultivating intimacy and strengthening the bond between you and your partner.

EXPLORING SHARED ACTIVITIES

In addition to conversation, video calls offer a multitude of opportunities for exploring shared activities and interests with your partner. Get creative and think outside the box when planning your virtual dates, whether it's cooking a meal together, watching a movie simultaneously, playing online games, or taking a virtual tour of a museum or landmark.

Engaging in shared activities allows you to create meaningful memories and shared experiences with your partner, strengthening your bond and deepening your connection in the process. So, don't be afraid to get creative and explore new ways of spending time together in the digital realm.

THE POWER OF PRESENCE AND PATIENCE

As you navigate the world of virtual connections, it's important to remember the power of presence and patience in fostering meaningful relationships. Be fully present and attentive during your video calls, and resist the urge to multitask or check your phone during your time together.

Take the time to truly listen to your partner, to engage with them wholeheartedly, and to savor the moments of connection and intimacy that you share. Remember, building a meaningful relationship takes time, effort, and dedication, so be patient with yourself and with your partner as you navigate the ups and downs of virtual romance.

EMBRACING THE JOURNEY

In the end, the journey of nurturing chemistry through video calls is as much about the process as it is about the destination. Embrace the ups and downs, the laughter and tears, and the moments of connection and vulnerability that you share with your partner along the way.

Be open to new experiences, growth, and change, and trust that the bonds you forge through virtual interactions have the power to transcend physical distance and stand the test of time. So, lean into the magic of video calls, dear reader, and let them be a source of light, love, and connection in your journey toward building a meaningful and fulfilling relationship.

CHAPTER 6
Meeting IRL: Transitioning from Online to Offline

Welcome to the exhilarating phase of your digital romance journey—transitioning from online interactions to real-life meetings. In this chapter, we'll navigate the exciting terrain of taking your relationship from the digital realm into the tangible world, exploring the intricacies of making that leap from pixels to palpable presence. So, fasten your seatbelts and prepare for the adventure as we delve into the art of meeting in real life (IRL).

NAVIGATING THE TRANSITION

The transition from online to offline interactions marks a significant milestone in any digital romance. It's the moment when virtual connections transform into real-world encounters, and the chemistry that has been simmering through screens has the chance to ignite into something tangible and profound.

But with this excitement also comes a healthy dose of apprehension and uncertainty. Will the chemistry translate offline? Will the connection be as strong in person as it was online? These questions are perfectly natural but remember, dear reader, that true connection knows no bounds and transcends the limitations of the digital realm.

SETTING THE STAGE FOR SUCCESS

Before diving headfirst into your first real-life meeting, it's essential to set the stage for success. Start by choosing a comfortable and familiar location where you both feel at ease—a cozy café, a scenic park, or a bustling city square. opt for a public setting for safety and security, especially if you're meeting for the first time.

Communicate openly and honestly with your partner about your expectations, preferences, and boundaries for the meeting. Discuss logistics such as timing, transportation, and duration, and be flexible and accommodating to each other's needs and schedules.

MANAGING EXPECTATIONS

As you prepare to meet your digital love interest in person, it's crucial to manage your expectations and approach the encounter with an open mind and an open heart. Remember that real-life chemistry may differ from the virtual spark you've experienced online, and that's perfectly okay.

Be prepared for the possibility of nerves, awkward moments, and unexpected surprises, but also be open to the potential for magic, connection, and genuine intimacy. Keep an open mind and embrace the journey, knowing that every moment —whether exhilarating or challenging—is an opportunity for growth and discovery.

THE FIRST MEETING: MAKING A MEMORABLE IMPRESSION

When the moment finally arrives for your first real-life meeting, take a deep breath, and remind yourself to relax and enjoy the experience. Start by greeting your partner with warmth and enthusiasm, and let your genuine excitement and affection shine through in your interactions.

Engage in meaningful conversation, share stories and experiences, and be attentive and present in the moment. Pay attention to your body language and nonverbal cues, and strive to create a comfortable and welcoming atmosphere that fosters connection and intimacy.

NAVIGATING THE DYNAMICS OF IN-PERSON INTERACTION

As you navigate the dynamics of in-person interaction, remember to be respectful, considerate, and mindful of your partner's boundaries and comfort level. Take things at a pace that feels comfortable for both of you, and don't hesitate to communicate openly and honestly about your thoughts, feelings, and desires.

Be prepared for the possibility of differences and challenges that may arise during your first meeting, but approach these moments with patience, empathy, and a willingness to work through them together. Remember, dear reader, that the journey of love is not always smooth sailing, but it's the bumps and detours along the way that make the destination all the more rewarding.

EMBRACING THE JOURNEY

In the end, the transition from online to offline interactions is a pivotal moment in any digital romance—a moment filled with excitement, anticipation, and endless possibilities. Embrace the journey, dear reader, and trust in the power of connection and chemistry to guide you on your path towards love and happiness.

Be open to new experiences, new connections, and new adventures, and remember that true love knows no boundaries, whether digital or physical. So, take that leap of faith, meet your digital love interest in real life, and let the magic of human connection unfold before your eyes.

CHAPTER 7
Beyond the Honeymoon Phase: Sustaining Love in the Digital Era

Welcome to the chapter where love transcends the initial excitement and settles into a deeper, more profound connection—the phase beyond the honeymoon period. In this chapter, we'll explore how to sustain and nurture love in the digital age, navigating the challenges and joys of long-term relationships in a world that's constantly evolving. So, grab your partner's hand and join me as we embark on a journey of lasting love and enduring connection.

NAVIGATING THE TRANSITION

As the initial spark of romance gives way to a deeper, more mature love, it's essential to navigate the transition with patience, understanding, and commitment. The honeymoon phase may be over, but that doesn't mean the magic has to fade. Instead, it's an opportunity to cultivate a love that's resilient, enduring, and built to last.

CULTIVATING CONNECTION

In the digital era, maintaining a connection with your partner is more important than ever. With the distractions of technology and the demands of daily life, it's easy for couples to drift apart if they're not intentional about nurturing their relationship. Make time for each other amidst the busyness of life, whether it's scheduling regular date nights, taking walks together, or simply cuddling on the couch and enjoying each other's company.

COMMUNICATION IS KEY

Effective communication lies at the heart of any successful relationship, and in the digital era, it's more important than ever. With the convenience of instant messaging and social media, it's easy to assume that communication is effortless—but nothing could be further from the truth. Take the time to truly listen to your partner, to express your thoughts and feelings openly and honestly, and to communicate with kindness, empathy, and respect.

EMBRACING VULNERABILITY

In a world that often values strength and independence, it can be tempting to keep our vulnerabilities hidden away. But true intimacy and connection require us to be vulnerable—to open ourselves up to our partner, to share our fears and insecurities, and to trust that they will accept us for who we are, flaws and all. Embrace vulnerability as a strength rather than a weakness, and watch as it deepens the bond between you and your partner.

NAVIGATING DIGITAL DISTRACTIONS

In the digital age, it's all too easy for technology to intrude on our relationships, pulling our attention away from the ones we love and towards the endless stream of notifications, emails, and social media updates. Take proactive steps to minimize digital distractions in your relationship, whether it's setting boundaries around screen time, designating device-free zones in your home, or making a conscious effort to be fully present with your partner when you're together.

CULTIVATING GRATITUDE

In the hustle and bustle of daily life, it's easy to take our partners for granted and lose sight of the many ways in which they enrich our lives. Cultivate a spirit of gratitude in your relationship by regularly expressing appreciation for your partner and the little things they do to make your life better. Whether it's a heartfelt thank you for cooking dinner or a spontaneous love note left on the fridge, small gestures of gratitude can go a long way towards strengthening the bond between you and your partner.

EMBRACING GROWTH AND CHANGE

As individuals and as a couple, growth and change are inevitable parts of life. Embrace these transitions with an open mind and an open heart, supporting each other as you navigate the ups and downs of life's journey. Celebrate each other's successes, comfort each other through the challenges, and remember that love is not about standing still, but about growing and evolving together.

THE POWER OF RITUALS

Rituals play a powerful role in relationships, providing a sense of stability, comfort, and connection amidst the chaos of daily life. Whether it's a weekly movie night, a monthly dinner date, or an annual vacation tradition, rituals help to strengthen the bond between you and your partner and create lasting memories that you'll cherish for years to come. Find rituals that resonate with you as a couple and make them a priority in your relationship.

EMBRACING THE JOURNEY

In the end, sustaining love in the digital era is about embracing the journey—the highs and the lows, the laughter and the tears, the moments of connection and the moments of solitude. It's about showing up for each other every day, in big ways and small, and choosing to love and be loved, even when it's not easy. So, dear reader, embrace the journey of love in the digital era, and let it be a source of joy, growth, and fulfillment in your life.

CHAPTER 8
Love in the Time of Screens: Embracing the Digital Romance

Welcome to the chapter where love blossoms amidst the glow of screens and the click of keyboards—a testament to the power of digital romance in the modern age. In this chapter, we'll explore the unique dynamics and opportunities of love in the digital realm, navigating the joys and challenges of building meaningful connections through pixels and pixels alone. So, let's dive into the world of digital romance and discover the magic that lies within.

THE DIGITAL LOVE STORY

In an era defined by technology and connectivity, the landscape of romance has undergone a radical transformation. Gone are the days of traditional courtship and handwritten love letters—replaced instead by the immediacy and intimacy of digital communication. From swiping right on dating apps to exchanging heartfelt messages on social media, digital romance offers a wealth of opportunities for connection and companionship in the modern age.

NAVIGATING THE DIGITAL PLAYGROUND

In the vast and ever-expanding digital playground, navigating the waters of romance can be both exhilarating and daunting. With a plethora of dating apps, social media platforms, and online communities to choose from, finding your perfect match has never been easier—or more overwhelming. But amidst the noise and distractions of the digital world, there lies the potential for genuine connection and authentic relationships to flourish.

THE POWER OF CONNECTION

At its core, digital romance is about more than just swiping left or right—it's about forging meaningful connections with others in a world that's increasingly interconnected yet often isolating. Whether you're searching for your soulmate or simply seeking companionship and camaraderie, the digital realm offers endless opportunities to connect with like-minded individuals who share your interests, values, and passions.

EMBRACING AUTHENTICITY

In a world of curated profiles and carefully crafted personas, authenticity is a rare and precious commodity. Embrace the opportunity to be yourself in the digital realm, sharing your quirks, flaws, and imperfections with pride. Remember that true connection stems from genuine authenticity, and that the most meaningful relationships are built on a foundation of honesty, vulnerability, and mutual respect.

THE PITFALLS OF PERFECTION

In the age of social media, it's all too easy to fall into the trap of comparing ourselves to others and measuring our worth by likes, follows, and comments. But remember, dear reader, that perfection is an illusion, and that true love transcends the superficial trappings of online validation. Embrace your imperfections, celebrate your uniqueness, and remember that the right person will love you for who you are, flaws and all.

NAVIGATING DIGITAL BOUNDARIES

In the digital realm, establishing and maintaining boundaries is crucial for fostering healthy and fulfilling relationships. Whether it's setting limits on screen time, defining the parameters of your online interactions, or safeguarding your personal information and privacy, it's important to prioritize your well-being and protect yourself from potential risks and vulnerabilities in the digital world.

THE FUTURE OF DIGITAL ROMANCE

As technology continues to evolve and reshape the way we connect and communicate, the future of digital romance holds endless possibilities. From virtual reality dating experiences to AI-powered matchmaking algorithms, the digital realm offers a wealth of innovations and advancements that have the potential to revolutionize the way we find love and companionship in the years to come.

EMBRACING THE JOURNEY

In the end, love in the time of screens is a journey—a journey of discovery, connection, and growth in a world that's constantly changing and evolving. Embrace the opportunities that digital romance presents, dear reader, and let it be a source of joy, fulfillment, and companionship in your life. Whether you're swiping right on dating apps or sharing your heart with someone halfway across the world, remember that love knows no bounds, and that the digital realm is just another avenue through which it can flourish and thrive.

CHAPTER 9
Conclusion

Congratulations, dear reader, on concluding our journey through the digital landscape of love and connection. As we come to the end of this exploration, let us take a moment to reflect on the lessons learned, the insights gained, and the beauty of the human heart in all its complexity and depth.

EMBRACING THE DIGITAL ROMANCE

In the digital age, love knows no bounds, transcending the limitations of time and space to connect hearts and souls across the vast expanse of the internet. Whether you're swiping right on dating apps, exchanging heartfelt messages on social media, or nurturing a long-distance relationship through video calls and virtual dates, the power of digital romance is undeniable.

THE IMPORTANCE OF CONNECTION

At its core, love is about connection—connection with ourselves, connection with others, and connection with the world around us. In the digital realm, where screens and devices often dominate our lives, it's more important than ever to prioritize genuine connection and meaningful relationships. Whether you're forging new connections or strengthening existing bonds, remember that love thrives on authenticity, vulnerability, and mutual respect.

NAVIGATING THE CHALLENGES

While the digital era offers countless opportunities for connection and companionship, it also presents its fair share of challenges and pitfalls. From navigating the complexities of online dating to managing digital boundaries and avoiding the pitfalls of comparison and perfection, it's important to approach digital romance with mindfulness, intentionality, and self-awareness.

THE POWER OF LOVE

In the end, love is the greatest force in the universe—a force that transcends barriers, defies expectations, and binds us together in ways we never thought possible. Whether you're finding love in the digital realm or nurturing a relationship that's stood the test of time, remember that love is a journey—a journey of discovery, growth, and transformation that has the power to enrich our lives in ways we never imagined.

EMBRACING THE JOURNEY

As we bid farewell to this journey through the digital landscape of love and connection, let us carry with us the lessons learned, the memories made, and the bonds forged along the way. Whether you're embarking on a new romance, nurturing an existing relationship, or simply exploring the possibilities that the digital realm has to offer, remember that love is always worth the journey.

So, dear reader, as you navigate the twists and turns of the digital romance, may you find joy, fulfillment, and companionship in abundance. And may you always remember that in the vast and ever-changing world of the internet, love is the one constant that remains, guiding us on our journey towards connection, intimacy, and genuine human connection.

www.ingramcontent.com/pod-product-compliance
Lightning Source LLC
Chambersburg PA
CBHW070408230526
45471CB00006B/2710